The Midnight Ride of
Sybil Ludington

Marlene Pérez

Illustrated by James Watling
and Joe Lemonnier

Contents

Rigby
A Harcourt Achieve Imprint

www.Rigby.com
1-800-531-5015

All About Sybil

Sybil Ludington lived more than 200 years ago, but her bravery is still remembered today. When Sybil was born in 1761, the United States was not yet a country. At that time, Great Britain's King George ruled the 13 colonies of America. Sybil's family lived in the colony of New York in a town called Fredericksburg. Sybil had a large family.

Colonial Families Worked Hard.

- Most families lived on farms and raised their own food.
- People worked in the fields, operated mills, or made tools and other items that people needed.
- Families cooked food over an open fire and made things that their families used, such as candles and soap.

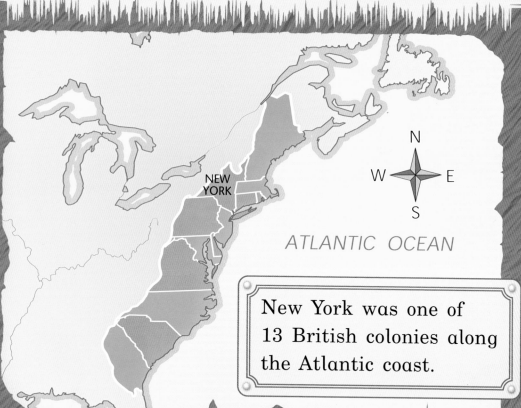

NEW YORK

N
W • E
S

ATLANTIC OCEAN

New York was one of 13 British colonies along the Atlantic coast.

Parents in the American colonies expected their children to help around the house. Sybil and other girls her age would help their mothers with cooking, mending clothes, and caring for their younger brothers and sisters. Sybil also had a very important job caring for her horse, Star. She had to make sure that Star got enough food, water, and exercise.

Sybil took care of her horse Star.

When there was time for fun, the children played games such as tag or hide-and-seek. An outdoor bowling game called "ninepins" was popular, too. When it was cold outside, people played indoor games like dominoes, marbles, and checkers.

Sybil's Father

Living in the American colonies in the 1760s was both exciting and scary. Many colonists thought that the British were not treating them fairly. These people, known as Patriots, believed that the colonies should become a country, free from British rule. They wanted to make their own decisions.

Sybil's father, Colonel Henry Ludington, was a Patriot. He had fought in the French and Indian War and was earning money by running a mill, where he made flour out of grain.

Some of his flour was used to make bread for the Patriots who had begun to fight the British.

Sybil knew that her father sometimes hid Patriots from the British. Sybil had taken food and blankets to the men hiding in her father's barn. She wanted to help her father free the colonies from British rule.

Sybil helped her father by bringing blankets to the Patriots he hid in the barn.

Colonel Ludington was in charge of the army in the area where he lived. The army was made up of volunteer soldiers who returned to their farms and families when they weren't fighting. The volunteers were called minutemen because they could be ready to fight "with a minute's notice."

Members of the Patriot army were volunteers who sometimes wore their own clothing.

The British soldiers were known as Redcoats because their clothing was bright red. The Patriots wore blue, but sometimes they wore their own clothing, like hunting shirts. Members of the Patriot army were not as well dressed as the Redcoats, but they were ready to fight. The Patriots gathered for training in a field which was near the Ludington's home. They wanted to defend their homes, while the Redcoats did not have the same interest in the war.

Fire in Danbury!

On the evening of April 26, 1777, someone on a horse came into the Ludington's yard with a message.

He carried the news that the British were burning the nearby town of Danbury. When Sybil looked outside, she could hardly believe what she saw. The sky was red with flames.

The British had a plan to quickly end the war by burning the supplies that the Patriots had stored in the area. They believed that an army without food and gunpowder would have to give up. Colonel Ludington knew that the British would try to destroy other supplies if the Patriots didn't stop them. He also knew that it would take General Washington's troops at least two days to reach Danbury. Colonel Ludington needed to stop the British right away!

Sybil's Ride

People in nearby villages had to be warned that the Redcoats were coming so that the Patriots could be prepared to fight. But who would carry the message? The man who had brought the message to them was too exhausted to continue on. Colonel Ludington had to stay at the farm to organize the soldiers as they arrived.

Sybil said that she would spread the news to other villages and farms even though she knew that the trip was dangerous. Both armies needed horses, so soldiers were robbing travelers on the road. What would happen if she met Redcoats along the way?

Because the messenger was tired, Sybil offered to spread the news that the Redcoats were coming.

Sybil's parents were afraid of the dangers that their daughter would face. But they knew that at the age of 16, Sybil could ride better than anyone in the village, and she could find the home of every soldier. Her parents finally agreed to let her go. Sybil found a warm coat, put a saddle on Star, and rode her horse into the darkness.

Sybil rode to every farm and village in the area. From the back of her horse, she banged on doors with a big stick, waking up the sleeping people inside. "Danbury is burning! Gather at the Ludington's home," she cried.

Sybil returned home early the next morning, exhausted from yelling her message to so many people. She had traveled nearly 40 miles warning the townspeople. This was farther than Paul Revere, a more famous rider, had traveled with his message about the Redcoats in 1775.

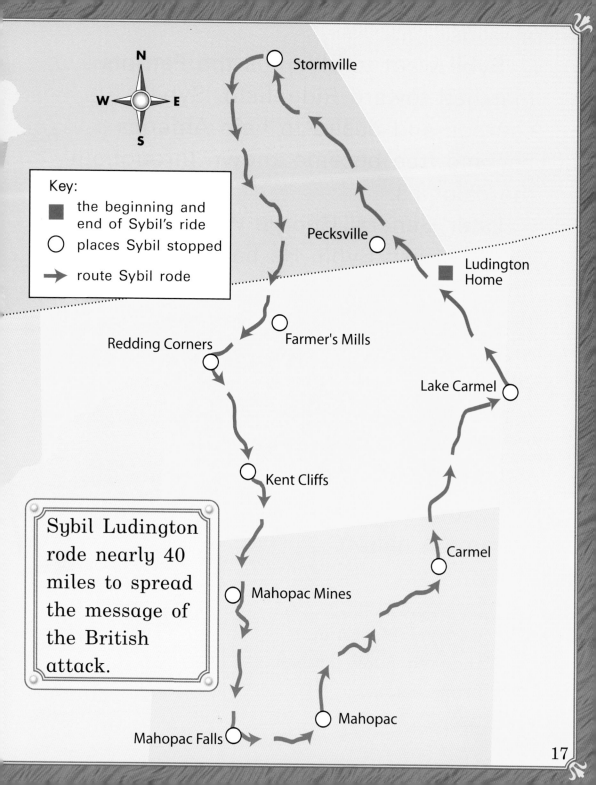

N
W · E
S

Key:
■ the beginning and end of Sybil's ride
○ places Sybil stopped
→ route Sybil rode

Stormville

Pecksville

Ludington Home

Farmer's Mills

Redding Corners

Lake Carmel

Kent Cliffs

Sybil Ludington rode nearly 40 miles to spread the message of the British attack.

Mahopac Mines

Carmel

Mahopac

Mahopac Falls

Sybil went to sleep as the Patriots marched toward Ridgefield. Sybil's courage and desire to help America become free became known throughout the colonies.

Later General George Washington came to visit Sybil. He had heard of her midnight ride and wanted to thank her for helping the Patriot army. Another famous Patriot, Alexander Hamilton, wrote Sybil a letter of thanks.

On October 19, 1781, the Patriots finally won the war. The United States of America became a nation.

General Washington thanked Sybil for her brave actions.

After the War

After the war ended, Sybil married Edmond Ogden, someone she had known as a child. Sybil's mother was only 15 when Sybil was born, but Sybil didn't get married until she was 23. Sybil and her husband had one son named Henry.

Sybil's husband died several years later. Although few women worked outside the home in colonial times, Sybil knew she needed to earn money to take care of herself and her son. Using the same bravery that she had shown on her midnight ride, Sybil opened a restaurant in Catskill, New York.

After Henry got married, Sybil moved with him and his wife to Unadilla, New York, where she lived until she died at the age of 77.

Remembering Sybil

A bronze statue of Sybil Ludington stands in Carmel, New York, to honor her brave ride. Her hometown of Fredericksburg is now called Ludingtonville in memory of Sybil's love of freedom.

For a long time, only a few people remembered Sybil's midnight ride. Then in 1976 the United States Post Office created a stamp honoring Sybil for America's 200th birthday. The stamp was one of a set created to honor people who helped America win its freedom during the Revolutionary War. Now many people know about the brave midnight ride of Sybil Ludington.

This statue reminds everyone of Sybil Ludington's brave ride.

Index